Letters to My Younger Self

Looking back to pay forward hard won wisdom

Emery Jordan

©2023 Emery Jordan
ISBN: 9798391771142 (paperback)
ISBN: 9798392224050 (hardcover)

All rights reserved. No portion of this book may be reproduced, stored in a retrieval system, or transmitted in any form or by any means—electronic, mechanical, photocopy, recording, scanning, or other—except for brief quotations in critical reviews or articles, without the prior written permission of the publisher.

Table of Contents

Dedication **6**

Preface **7**

Introduction **9**

Faith **11**
   Take 100% Responsibility for Your Life 12
   Determine What and Who You Believe In 14
   Integrity Matters 16
   Forgive 18
   Be Grateful... Everyday... In Everything... 20

Fitness **22**
   Be Healthy... Love the Body You Are In... 23
   You are going to fail... Learn something from it! 25
   Move... As much as possible 27
   Do something that scares you... Regularly... 29
   Take the next right step... 31

Fiscal Responsibility **33**
   Read... 34
   Save... 36
   Tithe... 38
   Lead... 40
   Grow... 42

Family and Friends **44**
   Develop Your Square Squad 45
   Make sure you're equally yoked! 47
   People are in your life for a reason, a season, or a lifetime... Choose wisely. 49
   Always be kind... But always tell the truth. 51
   It's okay to have boundaries... 53

Fun **55**
    If it's not a hell yes, it's a no! 56
    Dance... 58
    Learn you... Love you.....................................60
    Get a dog... or a cat... 62
    Make some goals... Then get busy doing them! 64

Give Back! **66**
    Help someone you can, everyday... everytime..............67

Epilogue **69**
Photos **70**
Bibliography **74**

Dedication

Dedicated to Dr. Mark Watson and Dr. Sherry Woosley, two people who taught me how to give and help someone, who could never help you back.

Preface

In May 1997, I graduated from high school. Not just any high school, but Indiana Academy for Math, Science, and Humanities, a magnet school in Indiana that is consistently ranked as one of the best high schools in the nation. As a kid from a poor area in Gary, Indiana, this graduation marked the beginning and the end of a journey that would expand my horizons, and forever change the trajectory of my life.

Those 2 years in Muncie, Indiana, living 3.5 hours from home, matured me in a way that I would have never gotten without the experience.

Moreover, those 2 years taught me what felt like a million things...
...how big the world might be...

...how I can vibe with someone who doesn't look like me, or come from my background...

...how much faith would matter to me...

..the kindness of strangers...

...how life keeps moving, whether you are ready for it to move or not...

...how to stay connected with the people that matter to you... And how to let go of connections that don't...

...why character matters more than anything else in evaluating a person...

But, more than anything, it taught me how to give, especially when someone has no hopes in paying you back, other than to pay their giving forward.

Fast forward 26 years, in January 2023, and I was asked to be the speaker of the Academy's high school graduating class of 2023. While I was both shocked and honored, (and a little surprised that I was their best option, lol...) I, of course, immediately said yes.

You may ask yourself - why are you shocked that they would ask? Well, to understand that - you must understand the Academy alumni, as a whole. Just in my graduating class, there are doctors, lawyers, New York Times bestselling authors, politicians, entrepreneurs, professors, and on, and on, etc...

Beyond just my class, in considering the 30-year history of the Academy, there are hundreds of graduates who have gone on to do amazing things in life.

So, here I am, a Senior Project Manager, an author of two small books, and a husband and a father, thankful to be selected, but wondering what I could tell a group of graduates that is entertaining, meaningful, and provide some wisdom to this newest set of alumni.

It is with that thought that the idea of this book was born. When I graduated from the Academy, while I was smart, I know that I was not wise. I thought I knew a lot more about life than I did. There are times that I wish that I could go back to that kid and share with him some of the hard-fought wisdom of life that I have gained in the last 26 years. Therefore, I am writing this book, to that kid... to the Alumni that I will be speaking to soon... and to any younger person looking for some wisdom about life.

As you will come to learn in reading this book, I'm an avid reader... Like 4 books a week reader... As I have begun to prepare for writing this book, I have been influenced in part by *How Will You Measure Your Life* by Clayton Christensen and *The Last Lecture* by Randy Pausch. In both books, the author is writing to encourage the reader to understand and apply the lessons and hard-fought wisdom that they have gained through their lives.

You will find this book is structured across 5 pillars, the 5 values I use to live my life - **faith, fitness, friends/family, fiscal responsibility, and fun**. In each pillar, there are 5 letters that will cover a multitude of topics, including career, fear, relationships, integrity, perseverance, and values among several others. Finally, there is one letter that was so special to me that I separated it, as I think of it as the overall theme of this book.

For the majority of my life, I have lived my life based upon the principle that I wanted to be a little better when I went to bed that night than when I woke up that morning. Moreover, as I entered life after being divorced, a period that I refer to as Phase 2 of my life, I added one to that principle that I wanted to use my life experiences to get better, not bitter. In the spirit of both of those thoughts, I hope that the letters and lessons I share in this book make you a little better, make you laugh, but more than anything, make you learn.

Thank you for taking the time to read these words.

Sincerely Yours,

Emery S. Jordan

P.S. - Please make sure that you take a moment to read the epilogue, so that you can see how your purchase of this book will help me help others!

Introduction

Dear Emery,

Thank you for taking the time to read this book! You have had a fun and crazy ride in the 43 years (so far), that you have been on the planet. You have had awesome highs and heart-breaking lows. You have accomplished some major things, but had some pretty big failures as well. On the whole, I'd like to think that we have done more good than bad, but there is definitely a ton of both in your years.

Just in case no one clued you in, 26 years from now, you are going to be asked to be a speaker at the Academy graduation ceremonies - I know, it's a shock to me too... But, they definitely asked you... And even said that you were their first choice. As a result, I (older me/you) had the idea to write you a set of letters that will represent some of the wisdom that I'd like to think that we have gained over these years.

Over the letters, you will learn about the good, the bad, the great and the ugly of what happens in your life thus far. I'm not going to spoil it, but you are going to be surprised with some of the way that things turned out. There are people who you will never talk to again after this day that seem like the biggest people in your world. Moreover, there are people who you have never met that will change and grow you in ways that you would never imagine.

Okay... I know that we both like spoilers, so here are a few...
- You are going to write, at least 3 books - I know, nuts, right? Especially since we barely got through writing papers.
- You are going to get 3 college degrees and be excited about each one!
- You are going to get your heartbroken twice, and both of them, while not 100% your fault, will be transformational for you.
- You will still not like alcohol and will never try drugs.
- You will still love oatmeal raisin cookies.
- I know that you think that are you strong right now because you can bench 225 lbs, but you will eventually use 315 lbs as a warm up weight for reps.
- And - you will finally own your dream pair of shoes, Air Jordan 11 Concordes!

See... There's a lot of good stuff ahead.

A couple other things, I'm not going to do that thing where I tell you to invest in companies, or people to avoid, etc... You aren't going to believe this, but you need both the good and the bad experiences to wind up being the man that you are today. But, my hope with these letters is that you will gain the strength to keep going when life gets tough, and that you can gather a little wisdom.

To help with that - at the end of each letter, I will give you a principle that I hope that you hold onto - a little thought that I hope will help impact you along the way.

I love you kid! Keep your head up.

Sincerely Yours,

Emery S. Jordan

Faith

Take 100% Responsibility for Your Life

No matter how bad it is, no situation is ever greater than you. You always have three options: you can change the situation, accept the situation, or change your mind-set on how you see the situation. And you have the power in your hands to choose whichever is best for you. Never allow something else or someone's opinion to become the title of your book. Ever.

Jo Malone[1]

Dear Emery,

June 17, 2020 is going to be one of the hardest days of your life. There are going to be a ton of highs and lows in the next 26 years, but that specific day will be one of your worst. You see, that's the day that you are going to get divorced. There is no sound that will ever prepare you for hearing the gavel in the courtroom when the divorce is final. It's going to wreck you in every possible way - spiritually, emotionally, financially, and physically. You are going to want to quit at life.

But, out of that horrible experience will come a lesson that will redefine your entire life. You see, you will read a book - *The Success Principles* by Jack Canfield[2], that will redefine everything in how you approach life. This book, and its related workbook, *The Success Principles Workbook* by Jack Canfield, both will walk you through the steps and inspiration necessary for getting to the success that you want in your life. In fact, both books start with the same first principle, the principle for this letter - **Take 100% responsibility for your life[3]**.

That principle - taking full responsibility - doesn't mean that bad things won't happen - because they will. But, by taking full responsibility, you are able to do something about those things.

The book outlines an equation:

$$E + R = O$$
Event + Response = Outcome[3]

What that means is, that independent of any event, your response will always have an effect on the outcome. Moreover, your thoughts, behaviors, and actions will have a direct consequence on how you experience anything - either good or bad.

This doesn't mean that everything that will happen will be your fault - because there are a lot of things that happen that you could have never prevented. But, the blaming, complaining, and excuse making that we used to do all the time never helped us get where we wanted to be, and it won't help you going forward either. To make it even more clear, **you will never reach your potential if you blame, complain, or make excuses about your situations - good or bad.**

You have already experienced some of this at a smaller scale. I mean, think about when you were taking English, and you were frustrated with writing papers - it wasn't until you stopped complaining and did something about it that things changed. You got the help that you needed to write a competent essay. The sooner that you can get up and move forward - the more success that you will have overall.

One other note, you will come across a lot of people who not only don't do this - but will criticize you for your positive outlook and/or willingness to move forward. We will talk about it later, but for now, just keep moving forward. Some of those same people are the ones that will be coming back to you to figure how they can get the successes that you will have accomplished.

Principle: Take 100% responsibility for your life. It's the only way that you will have the power that you need to change your life in the ways that you want.

Sincerely Yours,

Emery S. Jordan

Determine What and Who You Believe In

We all have what it takes, inside us. Trust yourself, trust your intuition. Don't let someone else be in control of your destiny, and don't not go after your passion because of fear. Look fear in the eyes and say, 'I am coming for you.'

Laila Ali[1]

Dear Emery,

As you know, we are a Christian. But, right now, your faith is based, in large part, on the fact that you were raised that way. I mean, you, basically, lived in the church growing up - in fact, there are several people who believe that you will eventually become a pastor when you are older... (Newsflash - as of right now, that hasn't happened, and doesn't seem to be in the cards - but you never know what God has in store, right?) At any rate, what I'm saying is that right now, your faith and what you believe in hasn't been seriously tested.

Yes, you have been through some trials and tribulations to get to where you are, but by in large, you have been around Christians your entire life.

Black Christians...
White Christians...
Baptist Christians...
Lutheran Christians...

But all Christians... And while there are some major differences in black and white churches, at the end... It also comes back to Jesus.

However, in the future, the very near future, your world will explode with diversity of opinions. You will be exposed to Christians who don't act like Christians, and several other faiths - including Islam, Judaism, Buddhism, and Wiccan among others.

Moreover, you will go through periods where you believe that you are supposed to do something, you have a dream, but you go through what Bruce Wilkinson calls the Wasteland, in his book, The Dream Giver[2]. This is a period where you will endure significant struggle, trials, and sometimes, true evil that is blocking your path. You see people who chose a different - less structured or principled - path benefit. You will question why you chose to do more than be ordinary, or have principles, or even have morals overall. You will think really hard about taking the easy way out at times...

But take heart! While it won't feel like it, these times are growing you - and hardening you. They are helping you more than you can ever imagine - because they are helping you determine what and who you believe in. And more importantly, why you believe in it. Not everyone will agree with you - in fact, with your principles, ranging from not drinking alcohol, to tithing, to treating others the way that God would want you to - even if they don't act like it, you will have several people who encourage you to do the easy thing - or the thing that doesn't align with your beliefs. However, as you have more of these challenges, you will be able to take the small victories that you have accomplished in previous moments to tackle and achieve bigger challenges.

You won't be perfect. You will have times that the easy path will be too tempting to ignore, and you will pay dearly for those choices. You will have regrets when you take those easy paths, because there will be pain that you experience, and people hurt that you know you could have avoided with different choices. However, more often than not, you will do the right thing, because it's the right thing - even when others are doing the wrong thing.

The basis for all of this is your faith. It will be tried and tested and will strengthen as you go through additional challenges. What you will come to learn is that despite the advice of many, life is pretty simple - and there isn't much grey. One of the hardest things about life is to determine what and who you believe in - and then sticking to those beliefs. But, the rewards for doing just that are so numerous that they are impossible to count.

Principle: Determine what and who you believe in... Then, live out those beliefs daily.

Sincerely Yours,

Emery S. Jordan

Integrity Matters

If you want to know the true DNA of a team, follow the coaching staff and athletes around all day. What one does some of the time, one does all of the time. It's called integrity. Integrity isn't about being perfect. Integrity is having perfect intention as regards to your personal mission statement. Integrity isn't something you can turn on and off depending on what social situation you're in. You either have integrity or you don't. It's like being dead or pregnant.

Valerie Kondos Field[1]

Dear Emery,

As you have seen already in life, sometimes people act differently in one situation compared to how they would in a different situation. Whether it is gossiping about people when they aren't in the room, or acting completely differently when different sets of people are in the room - all of them are integrity breaches.

Integrity is sometimes a touchy topic because it's what people often expect of others, but don't always display themselves. Stephen Covey said it best, "We judge ourselves by our intentions and others by their behavior."[2]

Integrity is also touchy because it gets tied exclusively to ethics or morals. In these situations, if the topic isn't one that a group often feels comfortable attaching to ethics or morals, then integrity becomes a topic that people don't want to discuss and clarify because it will make them uncomfortable, often extremely so.

Nevertheless, integrity is more than just ethics or morals, or not gossiping, or not acting differently around different people. Integrity is aligning your actions with your truth.[3] It's about being whole, and complete.[4] It's about living one single life in a positive way for which you can be proud. Even more than that, your integrity, or your character, "will ultimately determine if your brains, talents, competencies, energy, effort, deal-making abilities, and opportunities will succeed."[4]

So, as you see - your integrity matters. One of the main reasons that it matters is because it determines the wake that you leave with a person after they interact with you. The wake, as Henry Cloud describes it, is determined by the answers to the questions - what did he accomplish? and how did he deal with people?[4] The wake you leave also determines your reputation, and whether people are excited to work with or interact with you in the future. While results matter, Maya Angelou was right, "people will forget what you said, people will forget what you did, but people will never forget how you made them feel."

As you have already seen, and will continue to see, people with holes in their integrity may succeed for a time, but in the long run - they are often undone by

16

their integrity flaws. Whether it's that the results they delivered no longer matter because they have left such a wreckage in relationships, or they have pushed too hard for results and chose questionable methods that eventually come back to ruin them; over time, just like right now, there will be hundreds and hundreds of cases of talented, driven people who compromise their integrity in large and small ways to get a small victory in comparison to what they gave up.

Don't be that person. There is no result that is worth your integrity. None. We will talk about failing in another letter, but know this, it is better to fail with integrity than succeed without it. No matter how much you succeed without integrity, you will never enjoy it because of the paranoia of knowing how you got those results.

Principle: Integrity matters! Live your life in a such a way that when people think of you, they smile.

Sincerely Yours,

Emery S. Jordan

Forgive

Harboring unforgiveness is like drinking poison and expecting the other person to die; it's not hurting the one you're holding a grudge against, it's hurting you.

Karen Jensen Salisbury[1]

Dear Emery,

John Maxwell, an author whom you will come to **LOVE** soon, described your approach to be people the best... You believe the best about people[2], as a result, you practice both the Number 10 principle (you believe everyone you meet is a 10) and the 101 principle (you find the 1% of things that you can agree on, and give it 100% of your effort)[3], and for the most part - it works well, really well. You have already developed several crazy stories and experiences from just treating everyone like they are a 10.

Unfortunately, though, you will run into people who violate your trust, and who take advantage of you. In some cases, those people even don't take responsibility for their issues or the issues that they have caused for you. In both instances, you will have the great desire to retaliate - and because you have that ghetto in you, you will want to come back at them harder than what they are coming at you...

DON'T DO IT!!! As I mentioned in another letter, you always can choose how you react to any situation. And when those people do you wrong, forgive them...

What does it mean to forgive? It means that you give up "the right to demand that the one who hurt you pay you back or be made to suffer for what they've done."[4] It means that you set them, and yourself free.

You may be asking - why? Why would I forgive?

Here's the thing, there are a ton of reasons. First, holding on to anger keeps the wound fresh and open, and you will never get a chance to heal.[5] Second, by setting it aside, you get the ability to regain control of an experience where you felt like you lost control, which gives you the freedom to move on from the experience[6], and potentially the people involved.[4] Finally, God said that we have to do it... I mean, right in the Lord's prayer - forgive others, as he forgives you[7]...

But more than all those reasons, you have seen firsthand the bitterness, cynicism, resentment, and trust issues that people develop from failing to forgive others.

It's not easy to do... In fact, for some people and situations, it's, honestly, a daily decision that you are going to give to God and move on. For some situations, it's easier because you can remove and limit yourself from those people or situations that caused you the pain in the first place. And when that is possible, I highly suggest it. Forgiveness does NOT mean that you must give people access to hurt you all over again, in spite of what anyone may tell you. God didn't call for it, and I don't think that its wise.

Nevertheless, there will be some situations where, due to circumstances, you will have to continue to interact with the people that hurt you. In those cases, limit your interactions to exclusively what is necessary, and keep it moving. Even more, trust God to handle the situation and use it for you to learn. Even though it won't feel like it, remember, all things work out in the end for those that love the Lord.

And the coolest part of forgiveness, when you take the high road, is that sometimes the Lord will show you how you made a good choice. Some people call them Godwinks[6], and they are pretty cool.

Principle: Even when it is hard, forgive! It's the best thing that you can do for you, and for others when you are hurt.

Sincerely Yours,

Emery S. Jordan

Be Grateful... Everyday... In Everything...

Being thankful is one of the simplest, and yet most powerful, habits you can cultivate. By counting your blessings daily, you can begin to condition your mind to look for the good in everything around you. Soon enough, you'll unconsciously begin to see the bright side of things and feel better about life. You can't feel bad while you're feeling thankful. As simple as showing gratitude sounds, most people struggle with it. It's much easier to focus on burdens than on gifts; to devote your attention to the things you don't have, rather than the things you do have.
Vex King[1]

Dear Emery,

As we both know - you are a positive person. In fact, some would argue that you are as positive as it gets most of the time.

But, being positive and being grateful aren't the same thing. You see, while being positive is important, sometimes people will use positivity to ignore life's challenges. This positivity, which is called toxic positivity, is that Pollyanna-ish approach to just believe that things will get better, and shaming others who don't feel that way as well.

Gratitude is different, it is a way of life that alters our gaze.[2] It is the understanding that life owes me nothing and all the good I have is a gift, accompanied by the awareness that nothing can be taken for granted.[2] Gratitude literally changes what and how you see things. It doesn't make a bad day less bad, or a rough moment less rough, but it gives you the power to move forward faster.

The real truth is, as Jon Gordon says, "When you are grateful for things in your life, big and small, you always seem to find more things to be grateful about. Abundance will flow into your life when gratitude flows out of your heart."[3]

So, the next question is how can one be more grateful? Here are some good steps from Robert Emmons[2]:
    1. Find the Joy, Look for the Good
    2. Accept the Grace, Receive the Good
    3. Show Love, Give Back the Good

These are important steps because we live in a world where bad things happen, even to good people. There are billions of examples of bad things that happen to people that seemingly did nothing to deserve them. But, the key difference between those that are able to move forward in life, and those who become stuck is that they are able to find a lesson or a silver lining in the situation.

For example, as I wrote earlier, your divorce was one of the roughest moments of your life. However, without that day, this book would not exist. You see, as a part of your recovery from the divorce, you will decide to blog. That blog will be read by a book agent, who will ask you if you would be interested in writing a book - something that we both know that you had never, ever considered doing. This will be your 3rd book - and who knows, there could be tons more after this one. But, the only reason that this book exists is because in looking to heal from the pain, you followed the steps above to find a silver lining in getting divorced.

And this is just one of a ton of stories that can all be traced to that ability to be grateful, every day, in everything.

Principle: Be grateful, every day, in everything. It will change what you see, how you feel, and how you experience everything.

Sincerely Yours,

Emery S. Jordan

Fitness

Be Healthy... Love the Body You Are In...

Stop adjusting yourself to fit the desires of others – you're perfect as you are, right now.

At the end of the day, the only reason we're bothered by people who shamelessly stare is our assumption that staring means we are doing something wrong. It's extremely common for anyone who presents themselves in a way that contradicts societal norms to be stared at by people who strive to present themselves in a socially acceptable way. That doesn't mean you're doing anything wrong.

Jessamyn Stanley[1]

Dear Emery,

I know that I said that I won't give away much of the future - but you are going to be a big guy, pretty much your entire life. Right now, you aren't as solid as you will be in the future - thanks to a mutual love of weightlifting and peach cobbler/carrot cake - but you will always be big. What I would encourage you to be more than anything else, however, is healthy - in every aspect, physically, mentally, spiritually, etc.

As you have already seen in your life to this point, there will be people who associate beauty and health with being thin. However, being thin is not a singular marker of health. Moreover, there are so many different body types out there that there is not just one path to health. For example, you will meet unhealthy skinny people, extremely healthy large people, and everything in between.

When it comes to your body, first - move it! We will talk about this in another letter, but move - at least 3x times week. It doesn't matter how you move it - in fact, you will move it in a myriad of ways over the course of your life. Just move it.

Second, love it! You are God's masterpiece![2] He made you exactly the way that you are, with the passions that you have. If God wanted you to be smaller, he would have made you smaller. Look at your lineage, there are big, strong people everywhere. Furthermore, yes, there will be people who have commentary on your size for a negative - but there are also people who love you because you are a big lovable guy! Besides, let's be honest - you couldn't put all the personality that you have in a small package - it would never fit, lol!

Finally, learn it! You love sports - basketball, tai chi, yoga, baseball, softball, weightlifting, swimming, biking, etc... In participating in all those different types of sports, you will have the option to learn a little about your body with each experience. But, keep learning about it - read books, not only to learn your body mechanics, but to also learn how to help your body reach your goals.

You are going to do a lot of great things with this body that you have. In fact, you are going to do a number of things that people of your size don't normally do. You will be a role model for others because you don't let your size keep you from doing things that excite or interest you...

...Well, except for running. You will never learn to love running... Well, at least not yet... Who knows what comes with the future, right?

Principle: Love the body that you are in. Learn it, move it, keep it healthy - but love it. It's the only one that you are going to have.

Sincerely Yours,

Emery S. Jordan

You are going to fail... Learn something from it!

You have to be willing to fall short, miss a shot, or take a risk because chasing failure is more about who you're becoming than what you're achieving.

Chasing failure took me further than chasing success ever did.

Chasing failure is about giving your best to what you want to accomplish and being willing to live with the results.

Ryan Leak[1]

Dear Emery,

You have had a pretty good run of successes to this point in your life...

High school graduate from one of the best schools in the country...
Computer competition captain...
Color Guard captain...
Avid weightlifter and athlete...
Multiple time scholarship recipient...
State Debate Medalist...

...And you are going to have a ton more successes in your future.

But, the thing to remember is that each and every one of those successes were born out of a failure. In each and everyone of those successes, you were what Brene Brown calls a FFT (f'ing first timer)[2]. You didn't know what you were doing, you were a little worried, but you gave yourself grace, and moved forward. The cool thing is that once you move past the FFT, you get used to doing the new thing, and it becomes less of a challenge over time.

Moreover, here's the thing - no matter what you do, you are going to fail at something. Failure is a part of the process of succeeding. You do something, you try something, you fail, and then, you learn. It's called failing forward[3], and it's the true key of how to get anywhere that is meaningful in life. Dave Anderson said it well[3],

> *Failure is the hallmark of success. It can be the starting point of a new venture, such as when a baby learns to walk; it has to fall down a lot to learn the new skill. Failure is also the mark of success you've worked for. When a pole vaulter finally misses in competition, it shows how far he's come. That failure become the starting point for his next effort, proving that failure is not final!*

The key thing to remember about failing, is that you always want to fail forward. According to John Maxwell[3], here are the steps to failing forward:

1. Realize there is one major difference between average people and achieving people - their ability to move past failure.
2. Learn a new definition of failure.
3. Remove the "you" from failure.
4. Take action and reduce your fear.
5. Change your response to failure by accepting responsibility.
6. Don't let the failure from outside get inside you.
7. Say good-bye to yesterday.
8. Change yourself, and the world changes.
9. Get over yourself and start giving yourself.
10. Find the benefit in every bad experience.
11. If at first you succeed, try something harder.
12. Learn from a bad experience and make it a good experience.
13. Work on the weakness that weakens you.
14. Understand that there's not much difference between failure and success.
15. Get up, get over it, and get going.

I know that is seems like a lot of steps, but you can honestly boil it down to this...
You are going to fail... Learn something from it! And get moving!

If you do that, consistently - there is nothing that you can't do.

Principle: You are going to fail... Learn something from it! And get moving!

Sincerely Yours,

Emery S. Jordan

Move... As much as possible...

"Shit or get off the pot." Too many people are waiting to get shit set up just right so they can do the thing they are gonna do. It's time.

Ashton Kutcher[1]

Dear Emery,

Over the next 26 years, there are going to be about a million different approaches to physical health and exercise. People will be convinced that eating everything is healthy, eating nothing is healthy, and everything in between. Additionally, people will be convinced that their way of exercising is the best and only way to be healthy. Or that you just need the right outfit... Or shoes... etc...

At the end of the day, when it comes to most things in life, including exercise, you just need to move. Get up off the couch, chair, or bed, and find a way to sweat. It doesn't even have to be exercise, I mean, there is a study where housekeepers found out that their jobs, with all of the movement was a perfect way to get movement.[2] When it comes to exercise, whether you are playing basketball, weightlifting, swimming, bicycling, dancing, doing yoga, or anything else - the most important thing is to consistently move, at least 3x times a week.

Why does 3x times a week matter? Because 3x times a week is a habit![3] Yes, ideally, you would be able to exercise every day. But, realistically, as life goes on, that becomes less possible for any number of reasons. However, if you can exercise intentionally 3x a week, you will get the large majority of the benefits of exercise. In addition, you will be moving enough outside of exercise that you should not feel guilty for not moving enough.

While this lesson applies to physical exercise and health, it applies everywhere else in your life as well. If you have an idea for something, do a little research, but then move.

Try it out...

Ooch...

As defined by Chip and Dan Heath, ooching is to construct small experiments to test one's hypothesis.[4] There are going to be tons of times where you will be torn about a decision, or hesitant to try to new approach, or lamenting something that has gone wrong, or frustrated about something, any number of other situations- in those times, move... Try something.

You will never know if you are right or wrong if you don't move. Inertia is our natural tendency to resist change and keep things the way that they have always been. As you learned in Physics, an object at rest will stay at rest, unless acted upon by an outside force. So, nothing changes, unless you move.

Principle: Move... As much as possible. Nothing changes, unless you move.

Sincerely Yours,

Emery S. Jordan

Do something that scares you... Regularly...

Be bold. If you're bold you might royally screw up, but you can also achieve much more, so be bold. You've only got your reputation to lose and that's not important. It's much better to strive for something that seems impossible, that's quite nuts on some level. So be bold, whatever it is. Even if you work on a customer desk somewhere, ask yourself, how can I be bold? Find those small moments of boldness because they are everywhere.

Martha Lane Fox[1]

Everything you want is on the other side of fear.

Stephanie McMahon[2]

Dear Emery,

Dave Hollis said it best -

> *Fear is going to be the single biggest threat to your ambition for a better life. Fear of the unknown, fear of what other people will think, fear of failure, fear of not being worthy or ready for the audacity of your vision. Any and all of these versions of fear will arise on your journey. It's a guarantee.[2]*

He's 100% right! Think about it - every success or cool story that you have this far in life happened on the other side of fear.

Going to Indiana Academy...
Twirling a flag in the Color Guard...
Doing computer competitions...
Competing in Speech & Debate...
Being a Cheerleader Lifter...

No matter what it is, if it's cool - then there is a going to be a twinge of fear before you do it.

So, that's why you need to do things that scare you, regularly. Now, I'm not talking about stupid things - like that time we jumped a fence and got a post stuck in our foot (thanks - that still hurts these days...) - but I'm talking about challenge ourselves to live up to our life motto - To be better going to bed than I woke up that day.

Now, here's the thing, in doing something that scares you, you will need a plan, even if it's just a mental one, for how you going to move forward in doing those things - because good intention with no plan is a wish. Here's a plan for how to move forward, from a great book, Do It Scared:[3]

    1. Claim Your Target

2. Find Your Why
3. Create Your Action Plan
4. Form Your Own Truth Club
5. Stop Comparing
6. Eliminate Excuses
7. Stay Encouraged

While we never had the words that explained it until seeing that list - it truly explains what we consistently do.

But, here's the other thing that you need to know. When you do cool, scary things on the regular, you are going to gather friends, fans, followers, and haters.

- Fans are people who will encourage you to rest on your past accomplishments and tell you that you have done enough.
- Followers are going to look for you to guide them to do what you have done.
- Haters are haters, they will find something negative to comment on what you did.
- Friends will continue to push you to be even better.

It's important that you connect with friends, help followers, celebrate with fans, and look for the helpful notes of haters. All those groups have a lesson to teach you - but you must not obsess over any group.

Finally, remember courage is not the absence of fear[4], it's moving forward despite the fear to do whatever you have set out to do. You are going to feel fear - before you do most things, especially cool things - but continuing to move forward and completing the task is what will set you apart.

Principle: When you attempt to do something of significance, you are going to be afraid. Do it anyway.

Sincerely Yours,

Emery S. Jordan

Take the next right step...

A year from now, you will wish you had started today. Start today. Time goes away and leaves us with only one of these two things: regret or results. A year from now you will wish you had unfollowed emotionally draining people. A year from now you will wish you had said 'no' more often. A year from now you will wish you had said 'yes' to yourself more often. A year from now, you will never be sure of the results. But you can certainly be sure of regret, if you don't start today.

Ankur Warikoo[1]

Dear Emery,

Martin Luther King Jr. once said, "Faith is taking the first step when you don't see the staircase." And while the first step is often the hardest one to take in starting a venture; sometimes when it comes to decision making, we get paralyzed to the point of not being willing to take any step for fear it is the wrong one.

Moreover, often people will look for paths of reasoning and explanation when it comes to decision making. If we can explain it, then we can know the why, connect it to a purpose - the decision feels like less of a risk, and makes more sense.[2]

It's often easy to decide when someone is choosing between a good option and a bad one, but it can be difficult when someone is choosing between multiple good or bad options. Or even worse, what do you do, when you don't know the next 5 steps down a path?

In those cases, take the next right step. Sometimes, that next right step is obvious and easy... But more often, that next right step is either murky or fear-inducing, or most often, both. In those times, it's more important to feel the fear, and do it anyway.

Why does it matter?

Because life will look different after you take that next right step.

You will have more information about the entirety of the path - either it was the right move, and you progressed.

Or it was the wrong move, and you learned something.

In addition, once you act, you will learn something about yourself. Is this pursuit one that is worthy of your time, talent, and treasure?

Finally, if you don't take the step - you will always wonder what could have been. Jim Rohn said it best –

> *We must all suffer from one of two pains: the pain of discipline or the pain of regret. The difference is discipline weighs ounces while regret weighs tons. There are very few pains as large as that of a missed opportunity, especially when you know that you could have done something different that could have affected the outcome.*[3]

In the world of improv, there is the concept of "Yes, And". This pillar of improv, requires participants to take the weirdest, wildest and craziest suggests, and respond - "Yes, And", instead of "No, But", to help create a scene.[4]

With "Yes, And", it doesn't mean that you will act on every crazy suggestion, but it gives every idea a chance to be acted on.[4] Similarly, by taking the right next step, you won't go down every single path, but you will give yourself every chance to experience the best that life has to offer.

Principle: When you aren't sure what to do, or where to go. Pray, then take the next right step!

Sincerely Yours,

Emery S. Jordan

Fiscal Responsibility

Read...

If there's just one piece of advice I could give, then I would urge people to foster a love of reading. It's our core skill as human beings. It's the gateway to everything else. It gets you involved. It allows your curiosity to follow its course. It connects us across time and space. Books and reading are the most important things. Yes, I would say above all else, I would urge people to foster a love of reading. Start as early as you can and keep on reading.
Bill Gates[1]

Dear Emery,

It's crazy to think how our passion for reading started - with the Pizza Hut Book It competition, and Donald J. Sobol's Encyclopedia Brown. We both know that we are a fat kid at heart, and the prize of those free personal pan pizzas was too much to turn down to just start and keep reading books. Since that time, we have just continued to expand the love... And yes, we have gotten some clunkers, but realistically reading has been a strong plus.

Going forward, double down on your reading! John Wooden said it best, "Five years from now, you're the same person except for the people you've met and the books you've read."[2]

By reading, you can and will learn new career paths, put yourself in position to learn and grow as a person, Christian, leader, partner, professional, athlete, and parent. It not a stretch to say that outside of your faith, reading is probably the single most powerful habit of your lifetime.

When you read, read everything...

Well, most things...

There's some stuff that you shouldn't mess with, but when it comes to reading - read it all!

Fiction...
Non-Fiction...
Faith...
Leadership...
Technology...
Sports...
Romantic Fiction...
Sci-Fi...
Mysteries...
Thrillers...
Biographies...
Etc...

By having such a diversity of reading, it helps you relate to more people, which is always a good thing. But, it also helps you learn lessons that you wouldn't learn any other way. It will also transport you to worlds and expand your thinking on a ton of different topics.

More important, it will help you become the connector and translator that you are meant to be. Given your passion for reading, you will be able to learn and teach yourself topics that help you lead and connect groups that would never intersect without your skill set. You have already seen that now - you have an ability to chill with some of anyone now - that skill only gets better when you have more knowledge of the world and continue to learn from others.

When it comes to reading, there isn't a golden number of books or a finish line that you will cross. You can always start slow - a book a month. But create the habit. When you continue to invest in yourself with books, it will only compound. The more you read, the more you will be able to read.

Finally, after you read a book - find a way to immediately apply 1-2 lessons from the book in your life. If you just read the books and never apply them, it is pointless, and you will forget the learnings. But, by simply applying 1-2 lessons, you will continue to do what we have always had as our lifetime goal - to go to bed better than what you woke up that morning.

Principle: Read - it's truly the key to your growth in every facet of your life.

Sincerely Yours,

Emery S. Jordan

Save...

The first idea – simple, but easy to overlook – is that building wealth has little to do with your income or investment returns, and lots to do with your savings rate.

Everyone knows the tangible stuff money buys. The intangible stuff is harder to wrap your head around, so it tends to go unnoticed. But the intangible benefits of money can be far more valuable and capable of increasing your happiness than the tangible things that are obvious targets of our savings. Savings without a spending goal gives you options and flexibility, the ability to wait and the opportunity to pounce. It gives you time to think. It lets you change course on your own terms. Every bit of savings is like taking a point in the future that would have been owned by someone else and giving it back to yourself.

Morgan Housel[1]

Dear Emery,

Of all the letters in this book, this is really the only one with a twinge of regret. You see, this is the only letter that we are writing that we really haven't lived as well as we would have liked. Partially because of growing up poorer than others, partially because we are extremely impulsive, and partially because there were times that we were trying to impress people that either didn't matter or didn't care about us, we have often spent money recklessly.

We didn't always waste it - there were times that we purchased things that had immediate value. It helped us in some way or was the technology fad of the moment. It provided us a service of convenience or comfort or speed that we would have not gotten otherwise. The thing is - often, whatever that item was, it would quickly outlive its usefulness, and find itself in a drawer or box, to be given away at some point in the future when we moved on to some other need of the moment.

But, if we could do it over - we would definitely save more. As Nigel Cumberland said, "Savings is the cornerstone of becoming wealthy."[2] While I don't know that we were ever worried about being wealthy, having a little more cushion for making good decisions would have been helpful.

As we are getting older, we have started to save some - but it has been a transition. First, it has required a shift in mindset - stuff is great, but experiences are greater. So, the first shift has been one of moving from acquiring stuff to acquiring experiences. This shift doesn't mean that there is not stuff worth buying, but it does mean that the things that are being purchased are for a distinct reason and usage. Moreover, the purchasing period is longer, and less impulsive.

Second, we had to put together a plan to save. The one that I have heard represented the most and the best is to live by the 10-10-80 method. The first 10%, or the tithe goes to God. We will talk about that later. The second 10% goes to a savings instrument - 401k, CD, something that is saving money in a place that you cannot immediately get to it. Finally, you live off the 80%. We aren't fully there yet - as of this writing - but that's the goal. If you can learn to live that way now, you will be so much better for it.

Finally, we have had to learn to 'only spend money that you have earned'.[2] This, honestly, has been the largest transition because it has required the largest adjustment. Between our FOMO (fear of missing out), and the availability of easy credit, whether credit cards or loans, we have been able to purchase whatever we want, whenever we wanted in some cases, and then try to figure out how to pay for it later. This, for us, as many, has led at times to a mountain of debt that we are working to get from under. It's a constant battle - one that we continue to fight now. We have had times that we have won, only to make bad choices and get buried again.

One other note, saving doesn't mean that you become a miser either. It's important to enjoy your life - you only get this one trip. One thing to always remember, money is a tool - it will allow you to do the things that are important to you. But it should never be more than that - a tool.

Principle: Money is a tool - save and manage it properly to gain access to the experiences that make life worth living!

Sincerely Yours,

Emery S. Jordan

Tithe...

I had to begin work as a small boy to support my mother. My first wages amounted to $1.50 per week. The first week after I went to work, I took the $1.50 home to my mother. She held it in her lap and explained to me that she would be happy if I would give a tenth of it to the Lord. I did, and from that week until this day, I have tithed every dollar God has entrusted to me. And I want to say that if I had not tithed the first dollar I made, I would not have tithed the first million dollars I made." The bottom line is that a giver cannot out-give God. My father's will directed the majority of his assets and holdings into a charitable foundation devoted to telling others the good news of God's love. As his son, I've never doubted that decision.

John D. Rockefeller[1]

Dear Emery,

This is going to be the most controversial letter in the book. I know - it seems crazy to say, but here's the thing, it's also going to be the most religious, which is going to make it the most controversial. But, in a different letter, I talk about determining who and what you believe in. You are a Christian, as a result, you need to tithe.

Tithing, as a practice, means that you give 10% to God. It actually means 10% of everything - your time, your money, etc. But most of the time when the topic comes up, it refers primarily to money. So, in essence, it means that you are giving 10% of your income to God - specifically, your first 10%.

On the surface, this should not be overly controversial, because it's one of the only places that God has essentially dared us in the entire bible. He says, that if given him the tithe, he will "pour down for you a blessing until there is no more need."[2] Moreover, he calls not tithing stealing from him - which is kind of a tough thing to live with.

This would make one believe that tithing should be an easy commitment to make. However, it is not. There are two major challenges that people who don't tithe have to work through.

One challenge is one of faith. It is the faith to give God what he has desired - before you pay other bills or handle other commitments. It is the faith to look at what you have and say I'm going to do what I can do, and let God handle the rest. Not only do most people struggle with that, but many Christians do also as well.

This leads to other challenge - the illusion of control. Here's the most controversial line in this entire letter.

Nothing that you have is actually yours.

Nothing... None of it. Even if you work for it, and buy it, it still isn't yours. It's all God's... His money, his stuff... He made us and owns it all. If you can understand that key topic, then it will break the grip that society will try to get you to have with stuff, including money. We are all just stewards - managers - of the blessings that God has given us.

This doesn't mean that you don't have to work... You have to work, because if you don't work you don't eat. But the actual blessings that are the fruit of that work are from God. As stewards, we must understand that we are just managing the property of another based upon their desires. As a result, when it comes to tithing, it's a measure of faith and understanding who is really in control. When you get that down, it is easy to tithe because you understand the source of the blessing, and that it isn't yours.

Principle: Give God his 10%... And see how he blesses you! He always keeps his word.

Sincerely Yours,

Emery S. Jordan

Lead...

The secret, darling, is to love everyone you meet. From the moment you meet them. Give everyone the benefit of the doubt. Start from a position that they are lovely and that you will love them. Most people will respond to that and be lovely and love you back and it becomes a self-fulfilling prophecy, and you can then achieve the most wonderful things.

Joanna Lumley[1]

A leader is a dealer of hope. Be a champion of what's possible today... inspire others to keep going, share a positive vision for the road ahead... most of all believe in others more than they believe in themselves.

Jon Gordon[5]

Dear Emery,

Outside of Jesus, John Maxwell will be the most influential leader for you in your lifetime. You will have several other leaders that will have significant impact on you - but John Maxwell is the most impactful, because he was the first - but also because many of the first things that you learned from him will guide the rest of your life. They became the foundation of your personal and professional career.

The first statement or lesson is:

Everything rises and falls on leadership.[2]

When it comes to leadership, there is no truer statement. Throughout life, both to this point and in the future, there are a myriad of examples of situations that have either improved or dramatically fell apart due to the leadership leading the situation. This applies in all areas of life - from business to sports to anything.

The second statement is:

Leadership is influence, nothing more, nothing less."[3]

Leadership, at its core, is the ability to influence someone to do what you are asking them to do. It is easy to confuse popularity with leadership, but they are not the same. Popular people can have the favor or approval of a people, but that doesn't become leadership until those favoring a person change their behavior because of the favored person's influence, actions or requests.[3]

Finally, the third statement is:

Leadership is a choice that you make, not a position where you sit."[4]

Another major mistake around leadership that people make is that they believe that they must have a title to be a leader. The reality is that while having a title may put a person in position to lead, often it is not available or required to be the leader in a situation. Remember - leadership is influence, nothing more, nothing less. And often, as you have already seen, the person with the most influence in an organization is not a person with a title.

One final note that I would add is that we both know that you are hard-wired to lead. You have been doing it your entire life. So, when in doubt, lead. This doesn't mean that you will always be the person in the front, sometimes leading means encouraging from the back. Sometimes, it's picking someone up when they fall, or patting them on the back from a job well done. Sometimes, it's just listening to someone when they are struggling.

Always remember,
> *This world needs leaders . . .*
> *...who use their influence at the right times for the right reasons;*
> *...who take a little greater share of the blame and a little smaller share of the credit;*
> *...who lead themselves successfully before attempting to lead others;*
> *...who continue to search for the best answer, not the familiar one;*
> *...who add value to the people and organizations they lead;*
> *...who work for the benefit of others and not for personal gain;*
> *...who handle themselves with their heads and handle others with their hearts;*
> *...who know the way, go the way, and show the way;*
> *...who inspire and motivate rather than intimidate and manipulate;*
> *...who live with people to know their problems and live with God in order to solve them;*
> *...who realize that their dispositions are more important than their positions;*
> *...who mold opinions instead of following opinion polls;*
> *...who understand that an institution is the reflection of their character;*
> *...who never place themselves above others except in carrying responsibilities;*
> *...who will be as honest in small things as in great things;*
> *...who discipline themselves so they will not be disciplined by others;*
> *...who encounter setbacks and turn them into comebacks;*
> *...who follow a moral compass that points in the right direction regardless of the trends.*

John C. Maxwell[2]

Principle: When in doubt, lead! Everything rises and falls on leadership, but leadership is influence, nothing more, nothing less.

Sincerely Yours,

Emery S. Jordan

Grow...

No matter what anyone says, just show up and do the work.
If they praise you, show up and do the work.
If they criticize you, show up and do the work.
If no one even notices you, just show up and do the work.
Just keep showing up, doing the work, and leading the way.
Lead with passion.
Fuel up with optimism.
Have faith.
Power up with love.
Maintain hope.
Be stubborn.
Fight the good fight.
Refuse to give up.
Ignore the critics.
Believe in the impossible.
Show up.
Do the work.
You'll be glad you did. True grit leads to true success.

Jon Gordon[1]

Dear Emery,

Most people don't know this about us, but one of our biggest fears is that we will get to the Pearly Gates of heaven at the end of life, and God will ask us why we didn't do more with the potential that we had. Even now, 26 years later, the Parable of the Talents from Matthew 25[2] still haunts us.

For those that are not familiar, Jesus tells a parable where a master calls his servants together before departing on a journey. To one servant, he gives 5 talents; to another, he gives 2 talents, and to the final servant, he gives one talent. After he is gone some time, he comes back, and asks each servant for an account of what they did with the talents they were given. The servant with 5 talents, earned 5 more. The servant with 2 talents, earned 2 more. But, the servant with only one talent buried it, and wasted it. The master called him wicked and lazy and gave his talent to the one who originally got 5 talents.[2]

While it took us forever to realize that talent in the story is a reference to money - not actual talent or potential, it should still be noted that the idea still applies, that we need to maximize the potential that we are given. The best way to maximize any potential that you are given, is to grow it.

Not only do we need to grow, but we need to be highly intentional about growing in just about any area. Growth means change, and John Maxwell said it best, "you cannot change your life until you change something you do every day."[3] In being intentional about it, you must have a plan that details the goals that you want to reach, and exactly how you will get there.

Over time, you will come across a ton of models for growth, and how to approach and apply it in your life. But Ken Blanchard and Mark Miller have one of the best and easiest to remember[4], to grow you must:

1. Gain Knowledge
2. Reach Out to Others
3. Open Your World
4. Walk Toward Wisdom

Not only does it actually spell **GROW**, but it really explains the process of growth well.

First, you must learn something - and go looking for whatever you want to learn. Then, you need to work with experts or people a little more knowledgeable than you in the area. Next, you must be open to listening and learning. Finally, you need to move towards this new learning in the area of growth that you are chasing at the time.

If you can follow those steps, and most importantly, do the work, then you will grow, and it will stick and compound. And we will be able to make sure that we maximize all the potential that God has given us!

Principle: Unreached potential is one of the worst feelings and parts of life. If you want to be what you are meant to be, you will have to grow.

Sincerely Yours,

Emery S. Jordan

Family and Friends

Develop Your Square Squad

The quality of your life ultimately depends on the quality of your relationships. Not your achievements, not how smart you are, not on how rich you are, but on the quality of your relationships, which are basically a reflection of your sense of decency, your ability to think of others, your generosity.

Esther Perel[1]

Dear Emery,

In addition to John Maxwell, Brené Brown will be another one of the most influential authors of your lifetime. While John Maxwell will teach you about the mechanics of leadership, Brené Brown will teach you the mechanics of feeling and emotion. One of those lessons that you learn from her is the idea of a Square Squad.

As defined by Brené Brown, here's the process of identifying your Square Squad:

> *Get a one-inch by one-inch piece of paper and write down the names of the people whose opinions of you matter. It needs to be small because it forces you to edit. Fold it and put it in your wallet.*
>
> *If you need a rubric for choosing the people, here's the best I have: The people on your list should be the people who love you not despite your vulnerability and imperfections, but because of them. The people on your list should not be "yes" people. This is not the suck-up squad. They should be people who respect you enough to rumble with the vulnerability of saying "I think you were out of your integrity in that situation, and you need to clean it up and apologize. I'll be here to support you through that." Or "Yes, that was a huge setback, but you were brave and I'll dust you off and cheer you on when you go back into the arena."*[2]

But, to have a Square Squad to identify, you must develop them first. And to develop them, you must be able to develop exceptional relationships[3]. Those relationships have the following six traits, according to Dr. Carole Robin[3]:

1. You can be more fully yourself, and so can the other person.
2. Both of you are willing to be vulnerable.
3. You trust that self-disclosures will not be used against you.
4. You can be honest with each other.
5. You deal with conflict productively.
6. Both of you are committed to each other's growth and development.

So, in order to have great friends, you have to be willing to be a great friend.

As we will discuss later, not everyone is meant to be your friend, but I would encourage you to treat everyone like they are a potential great friend, like they are a 10[4].

Why, you might ask?

Well, first, everyone wants to feel like they are somebody.[4] You have seen this firsthand - everyone desires to be relevant to someone, but some people feel like they aren't relevant to anyone. The more people that you can make feel like they are someone, the more they are willing to potentially connect with you in ways that neither of you could imagine.

Second, to earn the trust of someone to be vulnerable with you, you must go first. You will have to show the trusting behaviors that will give someone else the permission and understanding to know that you are a person that's worthy of being trusted. The best way to do that is invest in them as people - work to understand what people sing about, dream about, and cry about[5] - and share the same things about yourself. That's the vulnerability that will build connection over time.

Craig Groeschel, in one of his sermons, explains the concept of refrigerator friends. He calls them friends who could come into your house, open your fridge, and eat something - and no one would bat an eye.

Here's what he doesn't mention, is that when you have great moments in life - those people, your refrigerator friends, or your square squad, are the ones that you want to share those moments with - because they know the journey to the top of the hill of accomplishment.

Principle: Make sure that you invest in people to develop your Square Squad. They are the ones that will be there for all the moments that matter.

Sincerely Yours,

Emery S. Jordan

Make sure you're equally yoked!

"Unequally yoked" is a big biblical term for "Don't get with the wrong person just 'cause they fine and they got a few dimes." That's not worth it, because you will have a life of misery trying to go one way when he's going the other way. I mean, you'll literally begin to feel the distance. If one is moving and the other one is not, you're gonna begin to sense that tension.

Now, I know that may sound harsh, but think about it. Being yoked was a term used for oxen back in the day. The wooden beam that went over the oxen's necks was called a yoke. You would never put a strong ox next to a weak ox because the two wouldn't be able to achieve the goal of pulling a plow in a straight line without bringing strain on one and potentially damaging the other. So farmers tried to get two oxen that were compatible: "equally yoked." Being equally yoked allowed the oxen to achieve the goal.

Michael Todd[1]

Dear Emery,

According to Kate Rose[2] in her book, You Only Fall in Love Three Times, we each have 3 loves in our lifetime. They are:

Your Soulmate - who teaches you what is means to be in connection with another. It happens young, and normally is the stuff of fairy tales.[2]

Your Karmic Love - the hard love that teaches you about who you are, and how we want and need to love. This love hurts, through the tough lessons of lies, pain, and manipulation.[2]

Your Twin Flame - this is the love you don't see coming, as you are finally whole on your own, and this person complements and challenges us in the best ways possible.[2]

While it may be hard to believe now, given your palatial estate in the friend zone with most of the girls that you have met and/or been interested in dating to this point, you will experience each of these three loves. Even more, in between each of those loves, you will have a lot of girls that you are interested in dating - that will have no interest in dating you. And... There will be girls that are interested in dating you - that you will have no interest in dating.

You will go through periods where you wonder why you can't find someone, or you will chase after someone who is **ABSOLUTELY** wrong for you - in part, because you don't have a good method for selection. But, between those three loves, and the tons of books that you will read on love, women, and relationships, you will come to understand the other sex more in time.

I won't give away the future here - because each of those lessons are necessary for you to become the man that you will become, there is one principle that I want you to really internalize. It is imperative that you are equally yoked with whomever you date or choose into your inner circle.

Yes, it's a biblical term...

And yes, it will cause you to move on from relationships...

And yes, it will limit your ability to have fun - to a point...

But the people that you choose to date will all make an impact on you - positively or negatively. There are people that you dated even now that you feel bad about how things ended - but you should have never dated them. Not because they were bad people, but because you all were going in different directions with different beliefs and different intentions for life.

As Jon Gordon says, the person that you choose as a partner needs to be a person that gives you strength, who helps you raise your potential, and who supports you to become the best version of yourselves as you pursue your dreams and goals together.[3] This kind of support is impossible unless that person is as strong as you are and wants to grow as much as you do.

It will be tempting to settle - for someone who makes you feel good, or for someone who is willing to be with you, or for someone who is impressed with what you have done - but don't! As strong as you are - and you will get much stronger in the next 26 years - you will even get tired and worn out, and it is during those times that you are being carried that your partner's strength matters the most. It is during those times that no amount of flattery will provide you the support to do the tough, scary, and/or hard things that you need to grow in any way.

Finally, I know that right now being in the friend zone with girls all the time is tough - but I promise you, even that will be a benefit in time. You will be comfortable in spaces that other guys get goofy, you will be able to talk to people in a clear, concise, and respectful way - independent of their accomplishments, beauty, or resources. On top of all that, you will clearly know how to build relationships and connect with people - it will become your superpower!

Principle: When it comes to dating and relationships, make sure that you are equally yoked!

Sincerely Yours,

Emery S. Jordan

People are in your life for a reason, a season, or a lifetime... Choose wisely.

You do not lose relationships, you outgrow them. There's no code that says every person you come across is destined to stay in your life forever and ever. In fact, very, very few people will stay with you throughout the duration of your time here. This is not because you are too flawed to love. This is not because every relationship you have is destined to ultimately break down. This is because, over the course of your life, you will grow. You will change. You will be different.
Relationships will come into your life and they will run their course and they will change you in some important way and then they will pass.

You are not meant for the people who leave you, you are not always at fault for the people who have left, and you are not broken for those who have faded into the distance. Embracing the ebb and flow of life, and the impermanence of it all, is the way you will learn to love people when you have them and be grateful for them when you don't.

Brianna Wiest[1]

Dear Emery,

January 1, 2023 is going to be one of the best days of your life. As I said earlier, there are going to be a ton of highs and lows over the next 26 years, but that day will be one of the happiest.

You see, that's the day that you will get married to your Twin Flame[2] (we talk about that in a different letter). And while that day will mark the initial completion of a healing journey, what will make it most special is that it will be one of the first times that all the people that are important to you are in the room physically or spiritually.

You see, for the first time in your life, you will understand the true differences between the types of relationships in your life. You have always known that people are in your life for a reason, a season, or a lifetime - it has always been a struggle to choose wisely who goes where. But Dharius Daniels explains the types the best that you have ever seen[3]:

- **Friends** *are individuals who are relational assets and not liabilities. Friends are those whom God escorts into our environments because there is something they need to be for us in order to help us be what we need to be for him. Friends offer more than company; they help us carry out our calling.*[3]
- **Associates** *are people with whom you have periodic or consistent association. An associate is what I call a "tweener relationship." It is a category that describes a person who is not in the friendship category, but not in the assignment or advising categories either. A person should be assigned to the associate category when there hasn't been*

enough time, interest, or desire to develop the kind of connection required for friendship. It's a relationship where a person doesn't prefer to, for whatever reason, engage any deeper than the surface.[3]

- *Assignments are trainees, mentees, and/or advisees. This type of relationship exists primarily for the purpose of one person providing mentorship, guidance, training, and coaching to another. A key quality of the assignment category of relationship is that it is a lopsided exchange. Assignments are people in whom you will make deposits, but from whom you will more than likely not receive withdrawals. This doesn't mean assignments can't or won't make any contribution to our lives. It simply means the nature of the relationship is one that exists specifically for the purpose of you giving to someone what you may have received from someone else.*[3]
- *Advisors - we are their assignments! These individuals will serve as mentors and offer us guidance in specific areas of our lives, usually for a limited amount of time. We may have professional advisors in our career fields. We also may have spiritual advisors whom we allow to pour into us insight, wisdom, and direction. It's crucial that we recognize the advisors God has sent to us and not confuse them with other relationship categories.*[3]

The reason that January 1, 2023 will be one of the most meaningful, is that in addition to marrying your complement - someone who helped you feel whole. All your closest friends and family were in the room, including your amazing 3 kids. (Yep, you will have 3 kids, and they will be better than you, at least, than you were at their ages...) As a result of all your closest people being in the room, there was nothing but absolute joy that day.

Finally, one other thing to note - your twin flame will be someone that you have known for a long time. While you have known each other for a long time, it was the development in your relationship with one another along this spectrum from assignment to associate to friend to partner that you also cherish. You see, you were 100% not looking for a partner (you were most focused on healing) when you reached the point where you were able to realize that she was the perfect partner for you.

Principle: People are in your life for a reason, a season or a lifetime. Make sure you initially categorize them correctly - but always give the relationship room to grow. You never know what it might become!

Sincerely Yours,

Emery S. Jordan

Always be kind... But always tell the truth.

It is not the most masculine, macho, or the ones with the biggest muscles who win. It's those who look after each other, who remain cheerful in adversity, who are kind and persistent and positive. These are the characteristics that help you, not just to survive life but to enjoy it. And they're nothing to do with gender. The people who are successful are the ordinary ones that just go that little bit further, who give a little more than they are asked to, who live within that extra 5 percent.

Bear Grylls[1]

Dear Emery,

We talked about integrity in an earlier letter, but realistically, telling the truth is always important in every situation. Independent of whether the situation is one of a personal or professional nature, telling the truth is always the best thing to do.

Often, people avoid telling the truth because of a fear of either hurting someone's feelings or a fear of repercussions from the truth. But here's the rub, when the truth comes out (it always does...), the impact of not telling the truth and the resultant loss of trust is always worst.

The key when telling the truth is, to quote Patrick Lencioni, to tell the kind truth.[2] Instead of hitting someone bluntly with a difficult message, it's important to present it with kindness, empathy and respect. This doesn't mean that you sugarcoat the message, but that you do remember the words of Abraham Lincoln - "a drop of honey catches more flies than a gallon of gall."[3]

When it comes to having those tough conversations, it's important to recognize that you need to find the balance between grace and truth - a combination that Henry Cloud refers to as neutralized.[4]

Being neutralized means that having grace and truth together in balance counters the negative effects of having one by itself, which is especially necessary in times of truth telling.[4] Moreover, it's important to remember in these conversations, that you are not trying to or responsible for fixing someone. Your intent in telling the truth should be to reconcile and fix a problem. You can't fix a person, that's God's job.

One other final note about telling the kind truth - avoid absolutes, as much as possible. When I say absolutes, I mean terms like 'always' and/or 'never'. It is rarely true that someone always or never does something, but more importantly, when you use those terms, it is normally a trigger that will lead to a defensive reaction.

Those defensive reactions make it very difficult for your message to be received, even if it is neutralized.

Principle: Tell the truth... The kind truth, which is a balance of grace and truth... But always the truth.

Sincerely Yours,

Emery S. Jordan

It's okay to have boundaries...

The most precious, important thing that you have in your life is your energy. It is not your time that is limited, it is your energy. What you give it to each day is what you will create more and more of in your life. What you give your time to is what will define your existence. When you realize this, you'll begin to understand why you're so anxious when you spend your time with people who are wrong for you, and in jobs or places or cities that are wrong, too. You'll begin to realize that the foremost important thing you can do for your life and yourself and everyone you know is to protect your energy more fiercely than anything else.

Make your life a safe haven in which only people that have the capacity to care and listen and connect are allowed. You are not responsible for saving people. You are not responsible for convincing them they want to be saved. It is not your job to show up for people and give away your life to them, little by little, moment by moment, because you pity them, because you feel bad, because you "should," because you're obligated, because, at the root of it all, you're afraid to not be liked back. It is your job to realize that you are the master of your fate, and that you are accepting the love you think you're worthy of. Decide you're deserving of real friendship, true commitment and complete love with people who are healthy and thriving.

Brianna Wiest[1]

Dear Emery,

As we talked about in a previous letter, you should treat everyone like they are a 10, as a person - because everyone wants to feel like they are somebody.[2] But, the other side of that thought is that you need to also have clearly stated boundaries that define your expectations for people, and what you are and not willing to tolerate behavior wise from those that you interact with.[3]

A boundary can be defined as clear limits that establish around the ways you allow people to engage with you, so that you can keep yourself and your relationships healthy.[3] They show you where you end and someone else begins, which gives you a sense of ownership. This sense of ownership gives you the freedom and responsibility to determine the course of the relationship.[4] Finally, it is a cue to others about how to treat you.[5]

Boundaries can be porous, where they are weak or poorly expressed. They can be rigid, where they are like walls that keep others out. Or they can be healthy, where you are aware of your emotional, mental, and physical capacity, and are able to clearly communicate it to others.[5]

The reason that boundaries are tough is because they involve saying no to people, which most people don't always enjoy hearing. In fact, many people will chafe at hearing that word from you - because they will imagine that they are either entitled, deserving, or expectant that you will automatically fulfill their request.

The problem is, you cannot pour from an empty cup[6], and without boundaries the requests from others will greatly restrict your ability to not only reach your own goals - but also to properly ensure that you can take care of yourself.

When it comes to implementing a boundary, the simplest process was identified by Melissa Urban[3]:

1. Identify the need for a boundary.
2. Set the boundary using clear, kind language.
3. Hold the boundary.

It's important that this happens - because after you determine that you need a boundary, communicate it clearly, and then hold the boundary, you have done your part. The behavior of the person who is violating the boundary is not your responsibility, or something that you should feel guilty about.

As I said earlier, there are people who will not like your boundaries, and will imply that your boundary is hurting or harming them. This may be true from their perspective - but it is also important to remember that you are not responsible to harm yourself in any boundary area - physical, mental, emotional, intellectual, material or time[5] - or any area to aid someone else.

Remember, the word **no** is a full sentence. It's doesn't require any explanation.

Moreover, remember you always want to deliver any message with a blend of grace and truth - but the importance of a boundary helps communicate that truth.

Principle: It's important to have boundaries - in fact, it's a need, both for your self-care and to clearly define your relationships with others.

Sincerely Yours,

Emery S. Jordan

Fun

If it's not a hell yes, it's a no!

People think focus means saying yes to the thing you've got to focus on. But that's not what it means at all. It means saying no to the hundred other good ideas that there are. You have to pick carefully. I'm actually as proud of the things we haven't done as the things I have done. Innovation is saying no to 1,000 things.

Steve Jobs[1]

Dear Emery,

The ability to achieve anything is a true blessing. To this point, you have been an honors student, and graduate from one of the best high schools in the world. You have competed on computer competition teams during your summer and won several different awards.

The good thing about reaching these achievements is that you will have numerous opportunities and doors that will open for you. The bad part is that you simply cannot do them all - so you will have to so no to some things.

But, because you are a nice person, you will initially struggle with telling people no. You won't want to hurt feelings, or miss opportunities, or potentially burn bridges in your mind. So, like many others, will accept too much, feel stretched too thin, be busy but not productive, and overworked but not fulfilled. At this point, you will be ready to become what Greg McKeown calls an essentialist.[2]

An essentialist, according to McKeown, is someone is chasing the relentless pursuit of less but better.[2]

It's not just about saying no, but it is about pausing to ask, **"Am I invested in the right activities?"**[2]

An essentialist is not focused on getting more things done, they are focused on getting the right things done.

As you begin to determine to decide how to make those decisions, I would encourage you to think of the words of Walt Disney - find a job (or anything) that you like so much that you'd do it without compensation; then do it so well that people will pay you to continue."[3]

Or in more simple language - if something isn't a hell yes, then it's a no.

I would not encourage you to take this quote so literal as to only do things when you are paid, because there will be things you choose to do that pay you in something other than money, like joy, or love, or peace, or any number of other positive feelings. But, at the core, what you must do is to decide - why am I doing this thing that I have selected to do?

And if you don't like the answer, and you are not legally required to do it - then change your situation by stopping doing what you are doing.

Principle: Focus is the ability to say no to anything off-mission - and that's true freedom.[3] In order to have focus, something needs to either be a hell yes, or a no.

Sincerely Yours,

Emery S. Jordan

Dance...

If I was to give one piece of advice, it is this: life is all about rhythm. Your heartbeat, great sex, the seasons, how often you call your parents, your good days versus your bad days, your DNA, the universe, everything has a rhythm. You have to develop a well-stretched ear and listen. The more you listen for the rhythm of your life, the more you will hear it. Find your rhythm. Live your life to its beat.

Mickey Hart[1]

Dear Emery,

Whether it was gospel at church, or rap and Chi-town house on the radio, or the color guard, or steppin', you have always understood that there is a rhythm to life. Moreover, by truly connecting with, and losing yourself in that rhythm of a good song you can experience true momentary freedom.

So, with that said, dance!

Learn different styles of dance - Latin, ballroom, ballet, tap, hip hop, jazz, African...

Learn the cultures behind them, the expressions of feeling and joy in them, and truly experience the freedom that they all provide. Even learn the proper steps and cadences of them.

But, while you get into learning all the choreography and moves in each of the different styles of dance, learn to love the music first. Listen to it, feel the messages that it is working to convey. If it is a different language, try to learn the language, or translate the lyrics into English.

To truly dance and love dance, you will have to love the music, to find the intricate instruments and beats that separate one style from another, and then learn to move your body to those rhythms. To really let it hit your spine, and cause you to lose all sense of time, space, and company.

As you get better at dancing, you will eventually see, revere, and learn from professionals in all the different forms of dancing that you decide to experience. When you get to that point, it would be easy to get caught up in the status and specialties within each form of dance, to the point where you lose the essence.

Fight against that - do your absolute best to never lose the child-like wonder that comes from a great beat over a boombox when you are dancing in the bathroom.

Finally, when it comes to dancing, it will be easy to compare yourself to others - both at the beginning when you think you aren't that good, in the middle when you get better, and even when you are more mature, and are fairly good.

Don't do it!

In fact, comparison is the true thief of joy in all things, especially dance. To quote Samuel Beckett - dance first, think later. It's the natural order.[2]

Principle: In life, there are very few things freeing as a good beat that hits your spine the right way. When that happens, dance - enjoy the freedom of life.

Sincerely Yours,

Emery S. Jordan

Learn you... Love you...

Knowing who you are is the greatest wisdom a human being can possess. Know your goals, what you love, your morals, your needs, your standards, what you will not tolerate and what you are willing to die for. It defines who you are. I have learned not to obsess over being number one all the time. Sometimes not being number one gives you the incentive and the courage to fight harder; it is motivating. Have patience. Have grace. Be secure enough in yourself to base success on personal growth.

Beyonce Knowles-Carter[1]

Dear Emery,

While you have known the scripture for a lifetime, it is still hard for you to understand that you are God's masterpiece.[2] Not because you don't like you, but you don't always see yourself the way God sees you. Fortunately, or unfortunately, you are not the only person who has that issue.

As you have gotten older, you have become more emotionally intelligent - more able to understand and control yourself[3] - you have learned to love yourself and the ways that God made you, for the good and the bad. This learning really came to a head as you came to understand your purpose.

The biggest key to learning yourself and your purpose, has been the ability to describe both your strengths and weaknesses in common language without judging them.

For example, you have been loud your entire life. You were raised in a loud environment, and volume has always been a part of your life experience. This is not a good or bad thing - it is just a thing. As you get to the point where you can understand those kinds of traits without judgment, the better you are able to understand how and why you work the way that you do.

As you begin to assess and understand yourself - it will be important to approach this from different dimensions. While there are several dimensions to review yourself from, one of the better ones that we have seen is the SPHERES model by Mike Bayer[4]. Each letter in the world SPHERES represents a different dimension:

- **S**ocial Life
- **P**ersonal Life
- **H**ealth
- **E**ducation
- **R**elationships
- **E**mployment
- **S**piritual Life

As you learn about yourself, it's important to remember -

> *You are unique. No one could truly know what it has meant to walk in your shoes because only you have walked in them. Your sum experiences, thoughts, feelings, genetics, and spirit are yours alone. There has never been another you, nor will there ever be. You are no better or worse than anyone else, and even when you don't feel like you are anywhere near good enough, you are enough because of one simple truth . . . you are you. The only one.*
>
> *Mike Bayer*[4]

As you walk through each of those dimensions to understand yourself better, you will begin to see the special gifts, strengths, and weaknesses that God gave to you - how he wants you to use them to be better. This information is the key to understanding, internalizing, and walking in your purpose.

While I could tell you what we have learned our purpose is at this point, I don't want to rob you of the journey that you took to learn it - that journey is what made our life the joy that it has been!

Principle: You are God's masterpiece, and there is a plan and a purpose for your life. For you to learn it - you must take the time to learn and love yourself, first.

Sincerely Yours,

Emery S. Jordan

Get a dog... or a cat...

I rescued a horse and three dogs. After years of experimenting with antidepressants, meditation, hypnosis, and various forms of therapy, I realized that for me, animals are the easiest way to help me to feel calm, centered, and present. They've also taught me countless priceless lessons about boundaries, consistency, and discipline that I apply to my work and relationships every day. They are the best performance-enhancing drug I've come across, by far.
Whitney Cummings[1]

Dear Emery,

Since the days of Tabitha (your mom's cat that drove your dad crazy) and Peaches (that crazy stray dog that followed you on your paper route that you eventually adopted), you have always had random interactions with pets, but you have never really had your own pet, at least not until this point.

Part of the reason for that is just because you have never really had your own space - you have either lived with your parents - who never could agree on pets, or you have been living in an environment where pets weren't allowed for one reason or another. The other part of that reason, if we are honest with ourselves, is that between allergies and cost, we really weren't all that interested.

As I write this now, we are the owner of a labradoodle named Chance. While he's the second dog that we have purchased, he's the first dog that we have owned for more than a weekend. (The first dog, Minka, just didn't work out... lol...) As with all things, there are times that you love him, that you hate him, and have every emotion in between. He's like a furry kid who can't speak in a language that you always understand.

You got suckered into buying Chance by the kids, who said that he would be their dog - but that's not really the case.

He's your dog. He knows it, the kids know it, and while you hate admitting it to yourself, deep down inside, you know it too.

You have almost gotten rid of him numerous times, especially because he has a bad habit of destroying property that you love, and/or eating food that you have put aside for later, which he is proficient at "nose hustling" to find, and then figure out a way to get to it.

With that said, when you are able to do so, get a pet. Do your research on what makes sense for you where you are at that time. It may be a dog; it might be a cat - which have their own challenges - but do it.

As much as you want to strangle Chance, he has made your life exponentially better.

First, while you aren't one of those crazy dog people - he's cute and has opened doors to friendships that would have never happened otherwise. He literally knows no strangers and is the world's cutest icebreaker. He will be impossible to teach to fetch because he cares much more about the people and the dogs than he does about an actual ball or frisbee or stick. By taking him on walks and to the dog park, you will get into conversations with people who become friends, purely because he wanted to play with their dog.

Second, he will humble you to continue to think about people and things beyond yourself, which probably, no, definitely helps your decision making. Anytime that you have an impulse to do something, you will need to slow down to ensure that he has proper care - either a boarder or dog sitter, or something else. When you decide that you want to be lazy, he will cajole you into walking him because you know that he needs to get out to use the bathroom. He has helped build your confidence in your ability to take care of others - because there are times that you were certain that you weren't doing a good job, only to be told that you were, by the vet (he's a dog, he doesn't talk, lol...).

Finally, he will make you significantly more emotionally intelligent. He does that a ton of ways... He's pretty much always happy to see you, partially because you free him from his crate, but also because he seems to genuinely like spending time with you. Since he cannot talk, you must be more attuned into his signals for food, or potty, or just wanting some affection, or when he needs to get some energy out. Your learned ability to attune to him has made you a better friend, partner, professional, and person overall. He has also made you more self-aware because he seems to be able to pick up on everyone's emotions and deal with them accordingly. You have learned how to be more self-aware from him.

So, in the end, while he is a pain in the tail, he's a great dog. And based upon talking with other pet owners, the lessons that he has taught me are similar ones that they have learned as well.

Principle: When you can take care of it, get a dog... Or a cat... Or just about any pet. They will make you a better person.

Sincerely Yours,

Emery S. Jordan

Make some goals... Then get busy doing them!

There will be 'Aha!' moments in life when a light might go on, when you think to yourself, 'I MUST do that' – whatever it is. It's not because someone says you should do it, but it's because you feel absolutely compelled to and there would be something wrong with the world if you didn't. If you find that light – acknowledge it. Find other people who share that passion. Cultivate it. Find that deeper purpose in your life.

Annie Lennox[1]

Dear Emery,

I strongly debated about writing this letter because we have never really struggled with goals. I mean, when we have been determined to do something, we get it done. When we are truly motivated, there really aren't many things that will stop us from accomplishing a goal.

At the same time, when we aren't motivated, or don't have a clear direction - we can procrastinate with the best of them. In fact, whether it's using an excuse, or focusing on what you can't control, or giving into worrying about problems[2], when you are not motivated you are amazing at not only not meeting a goal, but declaring yourself okay or normal for not getting it done.

When you get to those unmotivated or unclear moments, here are a couple of tips on how to move forward!

First, shrink the change![3] As described by Chip and Dan Heath, the idea of shrinking the change is derived from that the finding the motivation to do something large can be daunting when we aren't motivated. But we can often find the motivation to do something small that can build into a larger effort, or begin to start a set of smaller habits that build into a larger change.

As an example, we will never feel like cleaning...

Ever...

Even when you marry someone who LOVES cleaning - you still will not feel like cleaning.

But, if you put on some music, and commit to finishing one chore.

Taking out the trash...

Or washing the dishes...

Or starting a load of laundry.

The momentum of starting will often get you going into something larger.

Second, use behavior design to prompt yourself into moving. In Tiny Habits, BJ Fogg gives a simple, but effective method for using triggers to change a behavior that we would want to change. His method is to:[4]

- **Find an anchor moment** - an existing routine in life that will remind you to do the new habit.
- **Pick a tiny behavior** – pick a new habit you want to do, but at its tiniest form that is super easy.
- **Celebrate** the completion of the new habit.

We have used this method multiple times to get into the habit of working out early in the morning. You will always prefer to be a night owl, but with some proper prompting - you have on multiple occasions retrained your body to get up and workout consistently at 5am. (It's true proof that miracles happen every day, lol!)

Finally, the most important thing is to remember to understand the why behind the initial thought behind the goal. Being able to answer the thought - "why did I want to do this in the first place?"[5] - will re-connect you to original dream that led to the goal, especially as you are working through the messy middle reaching any goal.

One last note - not every goal is worth completing. So, if you re-ask yourself the why question, and the answer doesn't make sense based upon where we are in the current situation - it's okay to walk away from a goal. Sometimes, the best use of time and energy is to not complete a goal that is no longer meaningful.

Principle: Understand the why behind any goal that you choose. Once you got the why - get moving, even if it slow going when you get started.

Sincerely Yours,

Emery S. Jordan

Give Back!

Help someone you can, everyday... everytime...

None of us should ever underestimate our ability to change people's lives. There is a direct cause and effect of what we do here and what happens there. But if you want to help, you have to actually do something. You can't just talk about it. My motto is 'If you want to make things happen, you have to make things.' Create an object, a slogan, a film, a little book, a badge, a hashtag, a Red Nose Day . . . make something so wonderful that it captures people's hearts and minds so they can't help but be dragged in and help. And even better, make it funny too. That's all I have ever done.

Richard Curtis[1]

Dear Emery,

In a couple of years, a movie entitled "Pay It Forward"[2], will be released that will provide language to an experience that you already had once, but will experience at least one other time in your life. The theme of the movie is based around a project where a teacher challenges his students that upon receiving a favor from one person to do a favor for three other people, instead of exclusively returning the favor to the person that provided the initial favor. The movie is great, and I won't give the story away here, but it has a great impact.

While the language "pay it forward" was not as common then, as it is now, you have already had one of 2 foundational "pay it forward" experiences in your life.

You may have noticed that this book of letters was dedicated to Dr. Mark Watson and Dr. Sherry Woosley - that was highly intentional, as they play highly influential roles in those experiences.

The first, actually just happened about two weeks ago. As you know, based upon your family's financial situation, you were not going to be able to go to your senior prom. Your parents didn't have the money for you to get a tux, and you weren't planning to go. Upon hearing this, Dr. Mark Watson, a professor from Indiana Academy whom you knew, but you never actually took a class with, gave you the money for a tux and to go to the prom. Upon your promise to pay him back, Dr. Watson told you to pay it forward, the first time that you had heard that term.

While you had always been a person of faith and prayer, this is the first time that we can remember a true, unfiltered Godwink[3] - a time where God made a little miracle happen right in front of you by answering a prayer in a clear and direct way, through what might seem like a coincidence. It led to one of our favorite sayings - "Miracles Happen Every Day!"

The second will happen when you come back to Ball State for graduate school. Through no true fault of your own, you will be put in a situation where you need a miracle to complete the coursework for your first Master's degree. Dr. Sherry Woosley, an advisor who became a true friend, would not only help you complete more than 22 hours of coursework in the summer to finish the degree. But would also give you an opportunity to help develop software that would become fundamental to the field of education well after you graduate. Moreover, she would become a close friend and advisor for most of the next 10 years. Similar to Dr. Watson, when you asked what you could do to repay her - she said the same, "pay it forward".

As a result of their efforts, you will dedicate your life to being generous, and helping others as much as you can in whatever ways that you can. And while you will have lots of ups and downs, will change careers multiple times, will move several times throughout the Midwest (to this point) - you will ultimately, often, leave people and organizations better than when you found them.

Principle: You have been blessed consistently throughout your life, but you have been blessed to be a blessing. Help someone everyone you can, every day.

Sincerely Yours,

Emery S. Jordan

Epilogue

Dear Reader,

Thank you for taking the time to read these letters! I hope that you found some enjoyment and some nuggets of wisdom in my principles and stories of a lifetime (so far) lived pretty well, I'd like to think.

As I mentioned in the Preface, your purchase of this book will help me accomplish two goals that are very important to me.

First, as I write this book, I'm the parent of 3 children - Jalen, Gabriella, and Jaxen - two of which will graduate from high school within the next 5 years. They have been and will continue to be the greatest accomplishments of my life. They are much better kids that I was at their age - and my hope is that they will choose to read these words upon their graduation - and learn from these lessons.

Second, and equally important to me, I was blessed to attend two amazing high schools, West Side High School in Gary, IN and Indiana Academy in Muncie, IN, in my opinion. Each of them imprinted on me significantly to become the man that I am today. As a result, I am committing to donate **at least 20% of the proceeds** (after the tithe) of this book to a scholarship fund to be developed and/or grown at both schools, **with at least 10% going to each school**.

It has always been my dream to develop a way to give back to those communities and pay it forward to honor those who have invest their time, talent, treasure, and touch into me. It is my sincere hope that this book will bless those students with a little knowledge, and the opportunity to experience post high school education to help them grow into who God meant them to be.

Thank you again for taking the time to read or listen to these words. But, even more, thank you for helping me the dream of invest in a future generation after me come true.

Remember - Miracles Happen Every Day!

Sincerely Yours,

Emery S. Jordan

Photos

Indiana Academy Senior Year Yearbook Photo

New Year's 2023 Wedding Day Photos

Family Photo at 2023 Wedding

Chance

Bibliography

Preface
1. Christensen, C., Allworth, J., and Dillon, K. (2012). How will your measure your life? Harper Business.
2. Pausch, R., and Zaslow, J. (2008). The last lecture. Hachette Books.

Faith

Take 100% Responsibility for Your Life
1. Reed, R., and Kerr, S. (2018). If I could tell you just one thing...:encounters with remarkable people and their most valuable advice. Chronicle Books, LLC.
2. Canfield, J., and Switzer, J. (2015). The success principles™ - 10th anniversary edition: how to get from where you are to where you want to be. Mariner Books.
3. Canfield, J., Hall, B., and Switzer, J. (2020). The success principles workbook: an action plan for getting from where you are to where you want to be. Mariner Books.

Determine Who You Are and What You Believe In...
1. Reed, R., and Kerr, S. (2018). If I could tell you just one thing...:encounters with remarkable people and their most valuable advice. Chronicle Books, LLC.
2. Wilkinson, B. (2009). The dream giver: following your God-given destiny. Multnomah.

Integrity Matters...
1. Kondos Field, V. (2018). Life is short, don't wait to dance: advice and inspiration from the UCLA athletics hall of fame coach of 7 NCAA championships. Center Street.
2. Covey, S.M.R. (2006). The speed of trust: the one thing that changes everything. Free Press.
3. Sudbrink, L. (2021). Leading with grit: inspiring action and accountability with generosity, respect, integrity and truth. GRITty Stuff.
4. Cloud, H. (2009). Integrity: the courage to meet the demands of reality. HarperCollins E-Books.

Forgive...
1. Jensen Salisbury, K. (2017). I forgive you, but...:3 steps that can heal your heart forever. Harrison House Publishers.
2. Maxwell, J. (2014). 25 ways to win with people. The John Maxwell Company.

3. Maxwell, J. (2007). Winning with people: discover the people principles that work for you every time. HarperCollins Leadership.
4. TerKeurst, L. (2020). Forgiving what you can't forget: discover how to move on, make peace with painful memories, and create a life that's beautiful again. Thomas Nelson.
5. Schwarzeneggar Pratt, K. (2020). The gift of forgiveness: inspiring stories from those who have overcome the unforgivable. Penguin Life.
6. Rushnell, S. (2006). When God winks at you: how God speaks directly to you through the power of confidence. Thomas Nelson.
7. ESV Bibles. (2008). ESV study bible. Crossway.

Be Grateful... Everyday... In Everything...
1. King. V, (2018). Good vibes, good life: how self-love is the key to unlocking your greatness. Hay House UK.
2. Emmons, R.A (2016). The little book of gratitude: create a life of happiness and well-being by giving thanks. Gaia Books.
3. Gordon, J. (2019). Stay positive: encouraging quotes and messages to fuel your life with positive energy. Wiley.

Fitness

Be Healthy... Love the Body You Are In
1. Stanley, J. (2017). Every body yoga: let go of fear, get on the mat, love your body. Workman Publishing Company.
2. ESV Bibles. (2008). ESV study bible. Crossway.

You're Going to Fail... Learn Something From It!
1. Leak, R. (2021). Chasing failure: how falling short sets you up for success. Thomas Nelson Books.
2. Brown, B. (2020). URL://https://brenebrown.com/podcast/brene-on-ffts/
3. Maxwell, J. (2007). Failing forward: turning mistakes into stepping stones for success. HarperCollins Leadership.

Move... As Much as Possible
1. Ferriss, T. (2017). Tribe of mentors: short life advice from the best in the world. Harper Business.
2. Heath, C. & Heath, D. (2010). Switch: how to make change when change is hard. Currency.
3. Vanderkam, L. (2022). Tranquility by Tuesday: 9 ways to calm the chaos and make time for what matters. Portfolio.
4. Heath, C. & Heath, D. (2013). Decisive: how to make better choices in life and work. Currency.

Do Something that Scares You... Regularly...

1. Reed, R., and Kerr, S. (2018). If I could tell you just one thing...:encounters with remarkable people and their most valuable advice. Chronicle Books, LLC.
2. Ferriss, T. (2017). Tribe of mentors: short life advice from the best in the world. Harper Business.
3. Hollis, D. (2021). Built with courage: face your fears to live the life you were meant for. HarperCollins Leadership.
4. Soukup, R. (2019). Do it scared: finding the courage to face your fears, overcome adversity, and create a life you love. Zondervan.
5. Meyer, J. (2020). Do it afraid: embracing courage in the face of fear. FaithWords.

Take the Next Right Step
1. Warikoo, A. (2022). Do epic shit. Juggernaut Books.
2. Freeman, E. (2019). The next right thing: a simple, soulful practice for making life decisions. Revell.
3. Rohn, J. (2017). The ultimate Jim Rohm library. Audible Books.
4. Leonard, K. & Yorton, T. (2015). Yes and: how improvisation reverses "no, but" thinking, and improves creativity and collaboration -- lessons from the Second City. Harper Business.

Fiscal Responsibility

Read...
1. Reed, R., and Kerr, S. (2018). If I could tell you just one thing...:encounters with remarkable people and their most valuable advice. Chronicle Books, LLC.
2. Pasha, R. (2018). 117 John Wooden Quotes That Will Change Your Life. https://succeedfeed.com/john-wooden-quotes/

Save...
1. Housel, M. (2020). The psychology of money: timeless lessons on wealth, greed, and happiness. Harriman House.
2. Cumberland, N. (2019). 100 things millionaires do: little lessons in creating wealth. Nicholas Brealey.

Tithe...
1. DeMoss, M. (2011). The little red book of wisdom. Thomas Nelson.
2. ESV Bibles. (2008). ESV study bible. Crossway.

Lead...
1. Reed, R., and Kerr, S. (2018). If I could tell you just one thing...:encounters with remarkable people and their most valuable advice. Chronicle Books, LLC.

2. Maxwell, J. C. (2008). Developing the leader with you / developing the leaders around you (Signature Edition, 2 best selling books in 1 volume). Thomas Nelson.
3. Maxwell, J. C. (2007). The 21 irrefutable laws of leadership: follow them and people will follow you. HarperCollins Leadership.
4. Maxwell, J. C. (2011). The 360 degree leader: developing your influence from anywhere in the organization. HarperCollins Leadership.
5. Gordon, J. (2019). Stay positive: encouraging quotes and messages to fuel your life with positive energy. Wiley.

Grow…
1. Gordon, J. (2017). The power of positive leadership: how and why positive leaders transform teams and organizations and change the world. Wiley Books.
2. ESV Bibles. (2008). ESV study bible. Crossway.
3. Maxwell, J. (2012). The 15 invaluable laws of growth: live them and reach your potential. Center Street.
4. Blanchard, K., & Miller, M. (2012). Great leaders grow: becoming a leader for life. Berrett-Koehler Publishers.

Family and Friends

Develop Your Square Squad
1. Reed, R., and Kerr, S. (2018). If I could tell you just one thing…: encounters with remarkable people and their most valuable advice. Chronicle Books, LLC.
2. Brown, B. (2018). Dare to lead: brave work. tough conversations. whole hearts. Random House.
3. Robin, C. (2021). Connect: building exceptional relationships with family, friends, and colleagues. Currency.
4. Maxwell, J. (2007). Winning with people: discover the people principles that work for you every time. HarperCollins Leadership.
5. Maxwell, J. (2010). Everyone communicates, few connect: what the most effective people do differently. HarperCollins Leadership.

People Are In Your Life for a Reason, a Season, or a Lifetime… Choose Wisely!
1. Wiest, B. (2022). When you're ready, this is how you heal. Thought Catalog Books.
2. Rose, K. (2020). You only fall in love three times: the secret search for our twin flame. TarcherPerigee.
3. Daniels, D. (2020). Relational intelligence: the people skills you need for the life of purpose you want. Zondervan.

Always Be Kind… But Always Tell the Truth.

1. Reed, R., and Kerr, S. (2018). If I could tell you just one thing...:encounters with remarkable people and their most valuable advice. Chronicle Books, LLC.
2. Lencioni, P. (2009). Getting naked: a business fable about shedding the three fears that sabotage client loyalty. Jossey-Bass.
3. Carnegie, D. (2016). How to win friends and influence people. Diamond Books.
4. Cloud, H. & Townsend, J. (2015). How to have that difficult conversation: gaining the skills for honest and meaningful communication. Zondervan.

Make Sure You're Equally Yoked!
1. Todd, M. (2020). Relationship goals: how to win at dating, marriage, and sex. WaterBrook.
2. Rose, K. (2020). You only fall in love three times: the secret search for our twin flame. TarcherPerigee.
3. Gordon, J. & Gordon, K. (2020). Relationship grit: a true story with lessons to stay together, grow together, and thrive together. Wiley.

It's Okay to Have Some Boundaries
1. Wiest, B. (2022). When you're ready, this is how you heal. Thought Catalog Books.
2. Maxwell, J. (2007). Winning with people: discover the people principles that work for you every time. HarperCollins Leadership.
3. Urban, M. (2022). The book of boundaries: set the limits that will set you free. The Dial Press.
4. Cloud, H. & Townsend, J. (2017). Boundaries updated and expanded edition: When to say yes, how to say no to take control of your life. Zondervan.
5. Tawwab, N. G. (2021). Set boundaries, find peace: a guide to reclaiming yourself. TarcherPerigee.
6. Media, C. N., & Audrey. (2021, June 21). "You Can't Pour from an Empty Cup": Why Self-Care Isn't Selfish. Modern Minds - Mental Wellness Practice, Charleston, Mt Pleasant, SC. https://modern-minds.com/you-cant-pour-from-an-empty-cup-why-self-care-isnt-selfish/

Fun

If It's Not a Hell Yes, It's a No!
1. Ferriss, T. (2017). Tribe of mentors: short life advice from the best in the world. Harper Business.
2. Mckeown, G. (2014). Essentialism: the disciplined pursuit of less. Currency.
3. DeMoss, M. (2011). The little red book of wisdom. Thomas Nelson.

Dance...

1. Reed, R., and Kerr, S. (2018). If I could tell you just one thing…:encounters with remarkable people and their most valuable advice. Chronicle Books, LLC.
2. Petras, K. & Petras, R. (2021). Dance first. think later: 618 rules to live by. Workman Publishing Company.

Learn You... Love You...
1. Couric, K. (2011). The best advice I ever got: lessons from extraordinary lives. Random House.
2. Tyndale. (2019). NLT life application study bible, third edition. Tyndale House Publishers.
3. Harvard Business Review. (2015). HBR's 10 must reads on emotional intelligence. Harvard Business Review Press.
4. Bayer, M. (2019). Best self: be you, only better. Dey Street Books.

Get a dog... Or a cat...
1. Ferriss, T. (2017). Tribe of mentors: short life advice from the best in the world. Harper Business.

Make Some Goals... Then Get Busy Doing Them...
1. Reed, R., and Kerr, S. (2018). If I could tell you just one thing…:encounters with remarkable people and their most valuable advice. Chronicle Books, LLC.
2. Selk, J. (2015). Organize tomorrow today: 8 ways to retrain your mind to optimize performance at work and in life. Da Capo Lifelong Books.
3. Heath, C. & Heath, D. (2010). Switch: how to change things when change is hard. Currency.
4. Fogg, B.J. (2019) Tiny habits: the small changes that make everything. Harvest.
5. Hyatt, M. (2018). Your best year ever: A 5-step plan for achieving your most important goals. Baker Books.

Give Back

Help Someone You Can Everyday... Everytime...
1. Reed, R., and Kerr, S. (2018). If I could tell you just one thing…:encounters with remarkable people and their most valuable advice. Chronicle Books, LLC.
2. Pay It Forward (film). (2022, August 30). Wikipedia. https://en.wikipedia.org/wiki/Pay_It_Forward_(film)
3. Rushnell, S. (2006). When God winks at you: how God speaks directly to you through the power of coincidence. Thomas Nelson.

Made in the USA
Columbia, SC
26 May 2023

1331d886-e3cf-461d-b043-55de371f16f9R03